The Corpus-Based

American English Pronunciation

Language Arts

Card

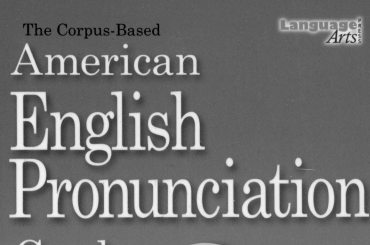

æ ʌ
ɑ ʊ
ɔ ʊ
ai ɔi

A Review of Sounds and Stress Patterns

Michael Berman

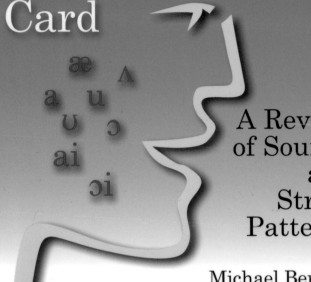

T0124030

Contents

The Vowels:

1. feet [i]	6. truck [ʌ]	11. dog [ɔ]
2. kid [ɪ]	7. hot [ɑ]	12. five [ai]
3. game [ei]	8. shoe [u]	13. down [au]
4. bed [ɛ]	9. book [ʊ]	14. boy [ɔi]
5. hat [æ]	10. boat [ou]	15. compare [ə]

The Consonants:

16. party [p]	24. food [f]	32. house [h]
17. beach [b]	25. valley [v]	33. man [m]
18. teeth [t]	26. think [θ]	34. nose [n]
19. desk [d]	27. these [ð]	35. king [ŋ]
20. chair [tʃ]	28. sun [s]	36. list [l]
21. June [dʒ]	29. zoo [z]	37. run [r]
22. cold [k]	30. ship [ʃ]	38. wait [w]
23. garden [g]	31. measure [ʒ]	39. you [y]

Grammatical Endings:	*Stress and Rhythm:*
40. –s endings	42. Word-level stress
41. –ed endings	43. Sentence-level stress

Vowels
The Front Vowels
feet[i] • kid[ɪ] • game[ey]
bed [ɛ] • hat [æ]

These vowel sounds are produced with the tongue forward in the mouth. For each vowel, the tongue is placed at a different height.

1. feet [i]
Practice
1. we
2. mean
3. either
4. Chinese
5. The three regions achieved peace.

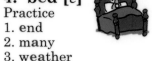

Contrasts

[i]	[ɪ]
1. seat	sit
2. feel	fill
3. least	list
4. seek	sick

5. I beat my brother.
I bit my brother.

2. kid [ɪ]
Practice
1. is
2. give
3. busy
4. women
5. It isn't permitted to begin until six-thirty.

Contrasts

[ɪ]	[ei]
1. it	ate
2. give	gave
3. kiss	case
4. liberal	labor

5. The pin is sharp.
The pain is sharp.

3. game [ei]
Practice
1. say
2. great
3. information
4. obtain
5. It's raining in Spain today.

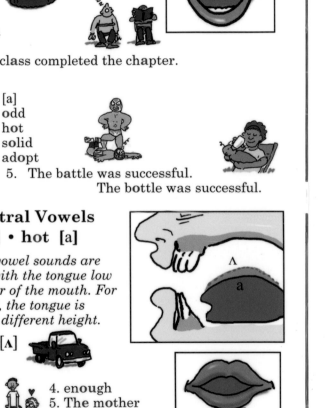

Combination Vowel:
The [ei] vowel sound (game) is actually a quick sequence of two different sounds. The tongue starts in a low position and then moves to a higher position. The shape of the lips also changes.

Contrasts

[ei]	[ɛ]
1. wait	wet
2. age	edge
3. main	men
4. trained	trend

5. Pass me the paper.
Pass me the pepper.

4. bed [ɛ]
Practice
1. end
2. many
3. weather
4. again
5. Extra effort will help you on the test.

Contrasts

[ɛ]	[æ]
1. head	had
2. guess	gas
3. set	sat
4. letter	latter

5. I like Texas.

I like taxes.

5. hat [æ]
Practice
1. ask
2. laugh
3. establish
4. perhaps
5. Half the class completed the chapter.

Contrasts

[æ]	[ɑ]
1. add	odd
2. hat	hot
3. salad	solid
4. adapt	adopt

5. The battle was successful.
The bottle was successful.

The Central Vowels
truck [ʌ] • hot [ɑ]

These two vowel sounds are produced with the tongue low in the center of the mouth. For each sound, the tongue is placed at a different height.

6. truck [ʌ]
Practice
1. us
2. does
3. come
4. enough
5. The mother loves her son.

Contrasts

[ʌ]	[ɑ]
1. nut	not
2. shut	shot
3. cup	cop
4. rub	rob

5. My luck was good. My lock was good.

7. hot [ɑ]
Practice
1. odd
2. job
3. father
4. beyond
5. Who is responsible for this problem?

5. Pass me the paper.

Contrasts

[ɑ]	[ɔ]
1. positive	pause
2. odd	audience

[ɑ]	[ou]
3. sock	soak
4. bottom	boat

5. Not that!
Note that!

The Back Vowels
shoe [u] • book [ʊ]
boat [ou] • dog [ɔ]

These four vowel sounds are produced with the tongue moved toward the back of the mouth. For each sound, the tongue is placed at a different height.

8. shoe [u]
Practice
1. do
2. June
3. fruit
4. through
5. The two assignments are due soon.

Contrasts

[u]	[ou]
1. grew	grow
2. too	toe
3. rule	role
4. boot	boat

5. The news was important. The nose was important.

9. book [ʊ]
Practice
1. put
2. took
3. should
4. understood
5. The woman could cook well.

Contrasts:

[ʊ]	[u]
1. full	fool
2. pull	pool

[ʊ]	[ɑ]
3. look	lock
4. good	god

5. Storms shook the airplane.
Storms shocked the airplane.

10. boat [ou]
Practice
1. no
2. goes
3. though
4. below
5. The old road is closed.

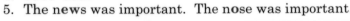

Combination Vowel

Contrasts

[ou]	[ʌ]
1. boat	but
2. most	must
3. tone	ton
4. phone	fun

5. The answer is known. The answer is none.

11. dog [ɔ]
Practice
1. off
2. August
3. draw
4. across
5. You ought to call the officer.

Contrasts

[ɔ]	[ou]
1. saw	so
2. caught	coat
3. lawn	loan
4. clause	close

5. Paul was called.
Paul was cold.

More Combination Vowel Sounds
five [ai] • down [au] • boy [ɔi]

Each of these vowel sounds is a quick sequence of two different sounds. The tongue starts in a low position and then moves to a higher position. The shape of the lips also changes.

12. five [ai]
Practice
1. lie
2. high
3. July
4. design
5. Mike has quite a wild life!

Combination Vowel

13. down [au]
Practice
1. now
2. power
3. allow
4. without
5. Our house is on the south side of town.

Combination Vowel

14. boy [ɔi]
Practice
1. oil
2. voice
3. toy
4. enjoy
5. Is the noise annoying?

Combination Vowel

15. compare [ə]
This sound (called the *schwa*) is the result of an unstressed vowel in a word. It is sometimes considered the "invisible" vowel sound because when it occurs between consonants, like in the word *compare*, it often sounds like nothing is there! When this sound occurs as the first or last sound of a word, like in the word *asleep*, it is a very short, quick sound made with relaxed lips and a relaxed tongue. It can also sound this way in the middle of some words, such as in *relative*. The [ə] sound can have many spellings.
Practice
1. asleep 4. after
2. support 5. relative 7. My cousin arrived
3. belief 6. reason seven days ago.

Consonants
Part I
party [p] • beach [b] • teeth [t] • desk [d]
chair [tʃ] • June [ʒ] • cold [k] • garden [g]

These eight consonant sounds, called "stops," are produced by stopping the air flow and then releasing it. The air is stopped by using different parts of the lips, tongue, teeth, and roof of the mouth.

Voiceless
16. party [p]
Practice
1. put
2. process
3. people
4. shop
5. Be prepared for important presentations.

[p] [b]

Voiced
17. beach [b]
Practice
1. big
2. body
3. object
4. globe
5. The boy's behavior is very bad.

Your Vocal Cords

The [p] and [b] sounds are produced using the same shape of the lips and the same stop-and-release air flow. **The difference between these sounds is in the vocal cords.**

- When making the **[p]** sound, the vocal cords do not vibrate. It is a "voiceless" consonant.
- In contrast, the **[b]** sound is a "voiced" consonant. This means that the vocal cords vibrate. If you put your fingers over your throat, you should be able to feel the vocal cords vibrate when you pronounce voiced consonants such as [b].

Contrasts

1. pack back	3. pin been
2. pace base	4. lap lab

You might have noticed two other differences between voiceless (pack) and voiced (back) sounds.
1. At the beginning of a word, voiceless consonants usually sound more explosive (they have a bigger puff of air) than voiced consonants do. Compare: *pace, base*
2. At the end of a word, the vowel before a voiced consonant usually sounds a little longer than the vowel before a voiceless consonant. Compare: *lap, lab*

Voiceless consonants: [p],[t],[tʃ],[k],[f],[s], [θ], [ʃ], [h]

Voiced consonants: [b],[d],[dʒ],[g],[v],[z],[ð],[ʒ],[m], [n],[ŋ], [w], [l], [r], [y]

Language Arts Press, LLC
P.O. Box 4467
Rockville, MD 20849 USA
(800) 313-7476
www.LanguageArtsPress.com

ISBN: 978-0-9791699-3-9

9 780979 169939

Voiceless	Voiced

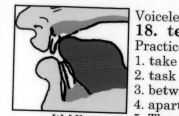

18. teeth [t]
Practice
1. take
2. task
3. between
4. apart
5. The student passed the test.

[t] [d]

19. desk [d]
Practice
1. day
2. difference
3. divide
4. broad
5. The director had doubts about the details.

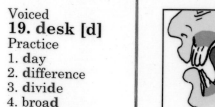

20. chair [tʃ]
Practice
1. chance
2. question
3. culture
4. catch
5. She chose the cheapest car.

[tʃ] [dʒ]

21. June [dʒ]
Practice
1. just
2. injure
3. age
4. edge
5. She enjoys her job as a judge.

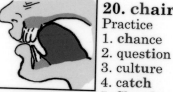

22. cold [k]
Practice
1. keep
2. close
3. quiet ([kw])
4. mix ([ks])
5. He quickly fixed the car.

[k] [g]

23. garden [g]
Practice
1. guess
2. agree
3. example ([gz])
4. drug
5. Don't give garlic to dogs.

Consonants, Part II

food [f] • valley [v] • think [θ] • these [ð]
sun [s] • zoo [z] • ship [ʃ] • measure [ʒ]
house [h] • man [m] • nose [n] • list [l]
king [ŋ] • run [r] • wait [w] • you [y]

These sixteen consonant sounds, called "**continuants**," are produced by a continuing flow of air. The air flow *is not stopped.*

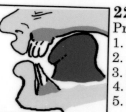

Voiceless	Voiced

24. food [f]
Practice
1. few
2. offer
3. telephone
4. enough
5. The fifteen flowers were a gift.

[f] [v]

25. valley [v]
Practice
1. value
2. of
3. cover
4. leave
5. My five favorite views are in Virginia.

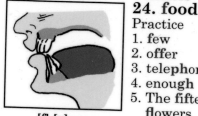

26. think [θ]
Practice
1. thank
2. thirsty
3. method
4. south
5. His birthday is on Thursday.

[θ] [ð]

27. these [ð]
Practice
1. the
2. though
3. other
4. together
5. The weather is rather cool.

"Th" Contrasts	[θ]	[t]	[θ]	[ð]
	1. theme	team	5. thesis	these
	2. through	true	6. thick	this
	3. thought	taught	7. tooth	smooth
	4. bath	bat	8. breath	breathe

28. sun [s]
Practice
1. said
2. sky
3. pencil
4. box [ks]
5. Six cents is all I've saved.

[s] [z]

29. zoo [z]
Practice
1. zone
2. size
3. easy
4. was
5. She has such blue eyes.

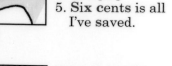

30. ship [ʃ]
Practice
1. show
2. sugar
3. issue
4. finish
5. Special machines count the votes in an election.

[ʃ] [ʒ]

31. measure [ʒ]
Practice
1. usual
2. pleasure
3. decision
4. garage
5. She traveled to Asia for the occasion.

32. house [h]
Practice
1. hat
2. here
3. who
4. behind
5. Heat it before you eat it.

[h]

[h] is the last voiceless consonant presented in this card. The rest are voiced.

33. man [m]
Practice
1. me
2. more
3. animal
4. time
5. Mary knows my name.

Out your nose!
[m], [n], and [ŋ] are produced by stopping the air flow in your mouth while breathing out your nose. For each of these sounds, the air is blocked in a different place in your mouth.

34. nose [n]
Practice
1. now
2. knowledge
3. into
4. begin
5. The ten new windows were expensive.

35. king [ŋ]
Practice
1. hungry
2. thank
3. strong
4. building
5. She sings long songs.

36. list [l]
Practice
1. life
2. family
3. little
4. tell
5. Your late arrival caused me trouble.

37. run [r]
Practice
1. red
2. write
3. river
4. appear
5. He was sorry for the poor results.

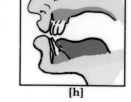

[l] vs. [r]

One of the most challenging contrasts among English consonants is that of [l] vs. [r]. Remember: For [l], the tongue touches the roof of your mouth. For [r], it does not.

Contrasts
1. light	right	4. collect	correct
2. load	road	5. Where is the file?
3. alive	arrive	Where is the fire?

38. wait [w]
Practice
1. we
2. quick
3. someone
4. away
5. My wife's advice was very wise.

Tip: Do not let your lower lip touch your upper teeth. Otherwise, you will pronounce the [v] sound.

39. you [y]
Practice
1. yes
2. young
3. onion
4. unusual
5. Have you used your jet yet, Joe?

Tip: Do not let your tongue touch your upper teeth or the roof of your mouth. Otherwise, you will pronounce the [dʒ] sound (June).

Grammatical Endings

40. –s endings

"Final s" endings are used in plural nouns (two *sandwiches*), third-person singular verbs in the present tense (he *gets*), possessive nouns (the *student's* book), and contractions (*she's* gone). Pronouncing –s endings correctly and consistently is necessary to deliver a clear, grammatical message.

The –s ending can be pronounced three different ways. The pronunciation depends on the sound that comes before the –s ending.

The –s ending is pronounced [iz] if the last sound of the word is [s] (*bus*), [dʒ] (*judge*), [z] (*prize*), [ʃ] (*rush*), [tʃ] (*reach*), or [ʒ] (*garage*). Note: This pronunciation of the –s ending adds another syllable to the word.
Practice
1. buses
2. judges
3. prizes
4. rushes
5. reaches
6. garages

The –s ending is pronounced [s] if the last sound of the word is [p] (stop), [t] (write), [k] (book), [θ] (month), or [f] (laugh). These consonants are all voiceless.
Practice
7. stops	10. months
8. writes	11. laughs
9. books	12. weeks

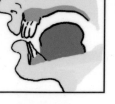

The –s ending is pronounced [z] if the last sound of the word is a vowel sound or if it ends in [b] (club), [d] (bed), [g] (bag), [l] (feel), [n] (win), [m] (seem), [ŋ] (sing), [r] (star), [ð] (breathe), or [v] (move). These consonants are all voiced.
Practice
13. grows	17. feels
14. clubs	18. wins
15. beds	19. seems
16. bags	20. sings

41. –ed endings

To write a regular verb in the past tense, we add –ed. These -ed verb endings can be pronounced in three different ways. The pronunciation depends on the sound that comes before the –ed ending.

The –ed ending is pronounced [id] when the last sound of the verb is [t] (wait) or [d] (add). This -ed pronunciation adds a syllable to the word.
Practice
1. waited	4. added
2. permitted	5. traded
3. celebrated	6. guided

The –ed ending is pronounced [t] if the last sound of the verb is [f] (cough), [k] (talk), [p] (drop), [s] (miss), [ʃ] (push), or [tʃ] (watch). These consonants are all voiceless.
Practice
7. coughed	10. missed
8. talked	11. pushed
9. dropped	12. watched

The –ed ending is pronounced [d] if the last sound of the verb is a vowel sound or if it ends in [b] (rub), [dʒ] (judge), [g] (beg), [l] (fail), [m] (blame), [n] (loan), [r] (ignore), [ð] (breathe), [v] (save), [z] (surprise), or [ʒ] (massage). These consonants are all voiced.
Practice
13. played	17. failed
14. rubbed	18. blamed
15. judged	19. loaned
16. begged	20. ignored

Stress and Rhythm

42. Word-level stress

In every word, one syllable receives more **stress** than the others. Stressed syllables are louder, longer and higher in tone than unstressed syllables. For example, in the word *teacher*, the syllable *teach* is stressed, and *–er* is not.

It can be difficult to know where to place the primary stress in many English words. However, there are some generalizations that can help you determine where the stress goes.

Compound nouns: Place the stress on the first part.
Practice
1. NOTEbook
2. CLASSroom
3. RAILroad
4. BUS stop

Numbers: The suffix "teen" (sixTEEN) receives the stress. The suffix "ty" (SIXty) does not. NOTE: In numbers with -ty suffixes, the "ty" is pronounced [di].
Contrasts
5. thirTEEN	THIRty	7. fifTEEN	FIFty
6. fourTEEN	FORty	8. sixTEEN	SIXty

Two-syllable nouns and verbs: Many two-syllable nouns and verbs share the same spelling. In these cases, the noun receives the stress on the first syllable, and the verb on the second.
Contrasts
	Nouns	Verbs
9.	PRESent	preSENT
10.	INcrease	inCREASE
11.	REcord	reCORD
12.	PERmit	perMIT

Reflexive pronouns: Words such as *myself* and *yourself* receive the stress on the second syllable.
Practice
13. mySELF	15. themSELVES
14. yourSELF	16. ourSELVES

43. Sentence-level stress

In sentences, the more important words are stressed and the less important words are unstressed.

Stressed words are often **nouns** (wood, book), **main verbs** (bring, read), **adjectives** (old, long), **adverbs** (quickly, slowly), and **negative expressions** (not, can't). These words are usually important to the meaning of the sentence.

Unstressed words are often **articles** (a, the), **prepositions** (to, for), **conjunctions** (and, but), and **auxiliary verbs** (have, can). These words are grammatically necessary but are usually not important to the meaning of the sentence.

Rhythm: A language's rhythm is its pattern of strong and weak sounds. In English, the rhythm is created by the stresses in a spoken sentence. The stressed words must stand out from the others in order to create a clear rhythm.

Practice
1.	MEN			DRINK		TEA.
	The MEN			DRANK	the	TEA.
	The MEN	have		DRUNK	the	TEA.
	The MEN	might have		DRUNK	the	TEA.
	The MEN	might have been		DRINKing	the	TEA.

Even though the number of syllables differs, the sentences above have the **same rhythm** and take approximately the same time to say. The unstressed words are shortened to fit the rhythm of the sentence.

Practice
2. She DOESn't PLAN to STOP.
3. His PROMise WON'T be KEPT.
4. He CAN'T underSTAND the TASK.
5. The FLIGHT to LONdon was CANceled.
6. I KNOW he'll be SAD when you LEAVE.
7. I DOUBT I can FIND my old HOUSE.
8. The MONey is LESS than she WANTS.
9. She's NOT going to TELL the poLICE.

Unstressed Words: As you have seen and heard, unstressed words are pronounced more quickly and softly (than the stressed words) in order to fit the rhythm of the sentence. Unstressed words can also be shortened in other ways.

Contractions:
10. MEN might've COME.
11. MARy's aWAKE.

Linking:
12. DRINK-it NOW! (Long form: Drink it now.)
13. CUP-a TEA (Long form: cup of tea)

Remember: Reductions are never written in formal writing. That is, reductions are for speaking, not for writing.

Reductions:
14. CREAM 'n SUGar (cream and sugar)
15. COFfee 'r TEA (coffee or tea)
16. TELL 'm NOW. (Tell him/them now.)
17. TELL 'r NOW. (Tell her now.)
18. JOE c'n DRAW. (Joe can draw.)
19. JOHN'S gotta GO. (John has got to go.)
20. THEY wanna EAT. (They want to eat.)
21. WE hafta LEAVE. (We have to leave.)
22. MIKE hasta PAY. (Mike has to pay.)
23. SHE'S gonna CALL. (She's going to call.)

The American English Pronunciation Card

Pronunciation Card: 978-0-9791699-3-9
Audio CD: 978-0-9791699-5-3
Card & Audio CD Set: 978-0-9791699-9-1
Also available:
Audio CD Download   Pronunciation Tutor Mobile App

For tips on using this Card, ordering information, and more, visit
www.PronunciationCard.com
or **www.LanguageArtsPress.com**

Language Arts PRESS